Tow Trucks

by Lola M. Schaefer

Consultant:
Lyndia S. Thomas
International Towing and Recovery Hall of Fame & Museum
Chattanooga, Tennessee

Bridgestone Books
an imprint of Capstone Press
Mankato, Minnesota

Bridgestone Books are published by Capstone Press
151 Good Counsel Drive, P.O. Box 669, Mankato, Minnesota 56002
http://www.capstone-press.com

Library of Congress Cataloging-in-Publication Data
Schaefer, Lola M., 1950–
    Tow trucks/by Lola M. Schaefer.
    p. cm.—(The transportation library)
    Includes bibliographical references and index.
    Summary: Describes the parts of a tow truck, how to operate them, and the work they do.
    ISBN 0-7368-0503-6
    1. Wreckers (Vehicles)—Juvenile literature. [1. Wreckers (Vehicles)] I. Title. II. Series.
TL230.15 .S34 2000
629.225—dc21   99-054149
                                                                                                          CIP

Editorial Credits

Karen L. Daas, editor; Timothy Halldin, cover designer; Sara A. Sinnard, illustrator;
    Kimberly Danger, photo researcher

Photo Credits

Archive Photos, 12, 16–17
International Towing and Recovery Hall of Fame & Museum, 14–15
Scott Gustavson, cover
Unicorn Stock Photos/Eric R. Berndt, 18
Visual Unlimited/Mark E. Gibson, 10
Waverly Traylor Photography, 4, 6, 20

1 2 3 4 5 6 05 04 03 02 01 00

Table of Contents

Tow Trucks

Tow trucks transport vehicles. People sometimes call tow trucks when their cars stop working. Tow trucks haul damaged vehicles from accident areas. Drivers use tow trucks to transport vehicles to be repaired.

transport
to move people or things
from one place to another

pulley

boom

winch

tow bar

wheel lifts

Parts of a Tow Truck

A tow truck has a truck body. The back of the tow truck has a long metal boom with one or two winches. The winches move cables through a pulley on the boom. A tow bar is at the end of the cables. Wheel lifts hang off the back of the truck.

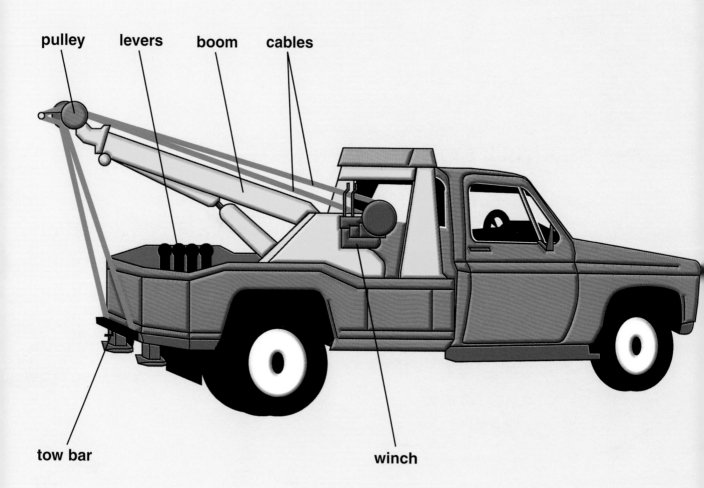

pulley   levers   boom   cables

tow bar

winch

How a Tow Truck Works

A tow truck's engine powers the towing equipment. The driver uses levers to move the winch. The winch moves the cables through a pulley on the boom. The cable lowers or raises a tow bar. The tow bar attaches to a vehicle.

Driving a Tow Truck

A driver backs up a tow truck to a vehicle. The driver loads the vehicle onto the lowered wheel lifts. Heavy straps hold the vehicle's tires in place. The driver then raises the wheel lifts. The tow truck pulls the vehicle after the wheels are lifted.

Before the Tow Truck

Mechanics traveled to stalled vehicles before tow trucks were invented. Mechanics fixed the vehicles by the side of the road. People used ropes and blocks with pulleys to pull vehicles out of ditches.

mechanic
a person who is trained to fix vehicles or equipment

Inventor of the Wrecker

In 1916, Ernest Walter Holmes Sr., of Chattanooga, Tennessee, invented the twin boom wrecker. Ernest put a shop crane on the back of a car. He then added a hand-cranked winch, ropes, and a hook. This wrecker pulled vehicles to his garage for repair.

shop crane
an overhead machine used to lift heavy items; mechanics use shop cranes to lift engines out of vehicles.

- - - - - -

Early Tow Trucks

Mechanics made early tow trucks in their shops. They used car and truck frames for the body. Mechanics added a boom, winch, and pulleys to each frame. Mechanics later replaced ropes with cables.

Tow Trucks Today

Today, people use several kinds of tow trucks. Small tow trucks pull cars and small trucks. Large tow trucks pull buses, large trucks, and motor homes. At airports, tow trucks pull airplanes.

Tow Truck Facts

- Some tow trucks are flatbeds. These trucks lift an entire vehicle onto a platform. Some flatbeds can tow two cars at one time.

- Tow trucks pull vehicles out of ditches. Drivers use large air bags to turn over tractor trailers that are on their sides. Tow trucks also use air bags to move airplanes back onto runways.

- Most tow truck drivers receive service calls on a computer in their truck cab. Other drivers use a truck telephone or a radio.

- Flashing emergency lights on top of tow trucks warn other drivers to pass carefully. Drivers sometimes place emergency lights on the vehicles they are towing.

Hands On: Work Less, Pull More

Tow trucks use winches to lift heavy vehicles. Winches work like pulleys. You can learn how to make a simple pulley. Pulleys make work easier.

What You Need

Small, sealed plastic bag
   half-filled with pennies
3 feet (1 meter) of string
Table
Empty thread spool
Chopstick
A friend

What You Do

1. Tie one end of the string tightly around the middle of the bag.
2. Place the bag on a table.
3. Try to lift the bag straight up with the loose end of the string.
4. Place the chopstick through the middle of the thread spool.
5. Have a friend hold the chopstick 12 inches (30 centimeters) above the table. One end of the stick should be in each hand.
6. Place the loose end of the string over the top of the spool.
7. Gently pull the string down and away from the spool. The spool acts like a pulley. You can lift the bag more easily with the pulley.

Words to Know

boom (BOOM)—a long pole that extends upward and outward; a boom supports a heavy object being lifted by pulleys.

engine (EN-juhn)—a machine that makes the power needed to move something

vehicle (VEE-uh-kuhl)—something that carries people or goods from one place to another

wheel lifts (WEEL LIFTS)—heavy metal bars on the back of a tow truck; wheel lifts raise and lower the wheels of the vehicle being towed.

winch (WINCH)—a machine made of cable wound around a crank that helps lift or pull heavy objects

Read More

Ready, Dee. *Trucks.* Mankato, Minn.: Bridgestone Books, 1998.

Rogers, Hal. *Tow Trucks.* Chanhassen, Minn.: Child's World, 1999.

Stille, Darlene. *Trucks.* A True Book. New York: Children's Press, 1997.

Internet Sites

Garrett A. Morgan Transportation Wonderland
http://education.dot.gov/k5/gamk5.htm
International Towing and Recovery Museum
http://www.towingmuseum.com
Tow Times Magazine Online
http://www.towtimes.com

Index